Fritz O.K.

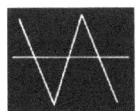

Trash Bird ©2019 by **Fritz O.K.** Published in the United States by Vegetarian Alcoholic Press. Not one part of this work may be reproduced without expressed written consent from the author. For more information, please contact vegalpress@gmail.com

Cover art by **Eleanor Hazard** www.eleanorhazard.com

For Emily McKern

1. DISCLAIMER ABOUT POEMS
2. (FUN)DAY BRUNCH
3. JUST NOW
4. BROKEN WHISTLE
5. AGONY IN DUX
7. A POEM CALLED BETH
8. MUDDIED UP THE WINGS WITH SHIT
9. THE RABBIT INCIDENT
10. THIS ONE CAN'T BE WASHED
11. COVER #1
12. FEELS LIKE LABORED BREATHING
14. JUST NOW
15. COMMUNICATION BREAKS DOWN FREQUEUNTLY
16. HOW TO DO IT
17. THE GUMSHOE VICE
18. PATCH OF WOODS
20. SINCE 1783
21. PRAGMATISM
22. I WILL WAKE UP TO A TEXT & HOOTS OF AN ALLEYWAY PIGEON
23. JUST NOW
24. LIKEWISE (FISH)
25. THE PARAMEDICS ACTED LIKE COPS
26. CONSIDERING THE WINDOW
27. PURSUANT TO THE CARD ISSUER AGREEMENT
28. ALBA
29. WE PREFER A MORE ORIGINAL PEST
30. THE DANCER
31. EXCEPTING THE PROCESS
32. RESTRAINT
33. SELF-HELP PORTRAIT
36. DON'T EVER CRY
37. NO LONGER SHOULD THEY DIG THERE
38. RUSHING THE UN-LOVE
39. THE RUM DRAIN
40. JERKING OFF ON THE WILDFIRE
41. HOPE IT RAINS SO JELLY BIRD CAN SWIM
43. REVOLUTION ON VIBRATE
44. NOTES ON AUTHORITATIVE VERSE

DISCLAIMER ABOUT POEMS

They are trash birds / Snapping
turtles and abortion doctors, gulping
at the bottom of the pond and
always busy.

The best that one can do is place these
soggy feathers one by one and
hold their breath.

And cover their genitals / And cover
their open heart.

(FUN)DAY BRUNCH

They're looking at fucking
Gatsby again. Touching him. Cradling
his balls with fuzzy tongues rolled out like
hot pink carpets.

And varying degrees of wetness.
And varying degrees of

      comprehension.

Sat down at the low chairs, thirsty
little fingers baked and dried, coarse and
brine to marinate a single hole.

Reaching for the wolf again. Rivers
under skirts / Rivers wrapped around
her toes and cloudy pigment. Strokes
against the current by the waterfall and

      almost children.

Looking at the fucking Twist again / With
only gentle pity. Grinding ivory
cock against a golden zipper.

Rivers turning green and
all new fragrance. They're screwing in
the bathroom now.

They're screwing in the bathroom now.

And varying degrees of fertility.

JUST NOW

Flipping through gazettes I found a
handful selling ghost work. Eastern meds
and all that *call your therapist.* Homemade
colonoscopies. A thousand fishbowl hickies
in a duplex.

I cannot seem to pinpoint my discomfort.
It pains me to imagine I have
missed the point.

BROKEN WHISTLE

It sounds like no one/s
having dinner.

An empty bath the
pink stains point

                    they laugh.

The pink stains laugh
and call in
another wacky bomb threat.

AGONY IN DUX

for CA Conrad

I'm pacing around the east wing
fast as California swims against her
ear and drowns again

      : this is the process about which
I would like to speak with the ones
in charge

the ones who got us pacing
to begin with—kings of college
clubs and skinny mannequin
dolls they never learned to sleep with
only finger stuff

who tried to make her long hard work a
doghouse / hard of
hearing

how they'd gone
replacing decent sex with
      eco-wars &
      tarot-pegging

not the least amusing writing
under pressure, swimming against
her fast &

losing out on not quite
finishing the sentence first
      but figuring
the point is something
useful / mother
listen to
      us

weeping over placing
footing awkwardly and
decidedly

      unnerved
about continuing to
pace
      without a
blueprint how to
float them : all the

nervous ones

A POEM CALLED BETH

There are packs of empty smokes and
some with just one left. Mostly empty. There
are cans of leaking sugar and some leaves. Mud
that dried and thin as chips. Mud that
won't betray the natural state of things. Receipts
and all that read like common tabloids, mathematics and
the string. There are greeting cards. Pink envelopes and
blue ones. Writing exercises and a broken
lighter. Pennies in a tiny cup from home. Bar codes,
bubble wrap. There are stains. There are at least
six olfactory profiles:

> *i: black tree*
> *ii: blue tree*
> *iii: green tree*
> *iv: L&M Red cigarettes*
> *v: heat*
> *vi: Pet Supplies stock room*

There is black and grey. There is carbon; there
are ashes. Thoughts of clean and re-
acquainting everyone

        to the dance

                slowly turning

silver again. Silver again and caked
in ash.

"It's only carbon," she tells me. "It only smells."

There are things in there I'd like to write of,
things I'd like to bury in a sandbox in a memory of
trauma. Things like rubber. Things like losing patience.

Things like rolled up dollar bills & six
hour flights. Seats leaned back & drunk &
drooling in my sleep. There are medicine bottles I
now use for marijuana, formerly Lorazepam, formerly
Flintstones Chewable Vitamins.

There are a lot of things in a *Poem Called Beth* and
I will write those things one day and I will read those
things and burn them /

Just to show it's mostly empty.
Just to show it's mostly lonely in the driver seat.

MUDDIED UP THE WINGS WITH SHIT

To stay for winter / huffing / huffing
every feather

                    oiled & drunk
                    oiled &

Unbecoming bird. Banded beak and
sliding in a womb.

Hard sometimes to breathe it only

        goes away to die.

THE RABBIT INCIDENT

for Olivia Case

Malachi stole everything but the nucleus, the floor-
Boards and his own misshapen tooth we had to glue
Back on at breakfast.

You wanted to preserve it in some gelatin. I wanted it
Shattered with a rock hammer and sprinkled over
Some canvas. Malachi wanted his face back. The thing had no
Barometer for excess.

I was drunk the night I marked him like a dog. No
Excuses. If I had been sober, for the floorboards, I would've
Marked him like a dog twice over.

This is just my testimony. That fucking thing was cursed.
And I simply don't have time to read a bible.

THIS ONE CAN'T BE WASHED

But it can fly some.

Sat among the garden steps with
clover mites, covering its
balls with the eventual fine-
tipped brushstrokes of a fairly un-
remarkable parasite.

Flies away to Brooklyn for a half a slice and
heard about a cosplay brothel somewhere in
the West Village. Will dress her as a spider and

Flies away to isolate the smells.

Give them bug spray. Give them more than
most the effort of an average tug.

Give them   clearing out the bathhouse.

                  empties any nest that can be washed.

Ditch the brush and come
down with a fist and
splatter.

Flies away to be with other
trash birds.

COVER #1

Many called us / unresponsive
pedals on a loose cover

pedals on a lonely nail.

We woke up on that afternoon &
split the grief in little cuts of bread &
honey / little dripping acts of wanting everything

       to stop ;; carrying on & splitting

All these flowers.

Every word is now a farce of nature.
Everything you say is desperate for a new response.

       pedals on a
       broken head.

FEELS LIKE LABORED BREATHING

is not there. what was before a neon shirt a
pizza box a glove

"some ice cream for the fatty with kid," he's saying

Starts running now Sherbet Blue
Starts fumbling for keys
Starts walking in a drum circle, fixing up a
ponytail starts all blue,
mismatched, marching with a ton and
something ( )
Starts with the iPod and paper
shorts
Starts every bloody scream of an emergency

+

Tell about the big hat, floating over
Sparhawk, the paper shorts double back and
whining of a scooter / slaughter of the pig
right there on Market

Starts the kotherfucking me-chains on
backpacks, the look into apartment
hallways the jog
Starts the spit performance, the hard sniff and
hair shake / church-walker talking all far moons
and foot dancers / flower on your frilly yellow
sundress

Starts the bike-streamer, starts shuffling out
here with chin problems, starts the feeling
the   rubbing hands together still hearing Market starts
the red bug / cup-drinker jingling a noose

The people speaking through them:

       tied-bag / neck-sweat

Cool sway and pin hats always
overdressed / bad singer with the beard-
walk / Live Free or super-soak the wheels a million
key holders, longboard gum chewer dancing
on a child's wing

This is Market: inside white fragment

buried in a lung.

JUST NOW

Perched on a cigarette, vomit in the
mouth an illustration / cum stains
in the henhouse never

        mattered.

COMMUNICATION BREAKS DOWN FREQUENTLY

In the morning birds
are yelping out
apocalypse.

I call back:

FUCK YOU!!!

And They respond
with just more
noise.

HOW TO DO IT

It's fairly simple: drink a ton & call
your local baker. Tell 'em you need mango cupcakes &
are capable of good ideas. Tell 'em how you've
grown since all the backlash, how you'll
take good care of Mom and Dad &
try to sound apologetic.

You won't be sorry, actually. You'll just pretend that
anything is possibly important. Wash your hands &
dial up the source. Intercept the mango shipment. Hold those
fuckers hostage till the baker tells you not to worry. Everything
is fine as we can hope for. Everything is golden brown &
wishing you were home again. Wishing they'd
forgive you is the source of all the mangos.

What's hard is you don't really want to do it. What's really
hard is every time they pat you on the back &
say it's worth the trouble.

Apologize & call another baker.
Drink a ton & forget I ever
tried to warn you.

THE GUMSHOE VICE

for Alex Davis

In the previous version the author probably dies,
probably dies for something silly like obsession or
someone like Nicoletta. Probably dies happy.

I don't really know. I wanted the birds to talk and
that's about it. I wanted him to boil his shoelaces and
be grossly, maddeningly in love. The opera mauve was
an afterthought. The South Wing needed decorations.

Nobody has to die for these things, X.
That's the truth. Every story is imperfect and
disgusting on its own. All that words can really do is

                                                  grind my teeth.

PATCH OF WOODS

i.

[I] stand on the stump with my stick.

[I] stare and scare away the robins.

[I] do grab an axe but because you tell me

    fucking manly men is back,
    is trending.

ii.

[I] walked and washed in the creek all morning

    terrified

  you watch me wash in the creek.

iii.

[We] prod around in mud and
    wetness

    and then am off my stump, off my
    speed make haste of recording
        you; you swirling down the
        street and chasing other rocks.
    These ones prettier.
    These ones to the absolute
    astonishment of March.

[We] will find something alive that
        lives here and   to swim with and

              are beaten to death"

iv.

[I] should not be here.

    the stone bench is
    ancient.
    the worms beneath are
    trying to sleep.
    the sticks will choke the dog and
    then what?

    definitive/un-
    definitive. With my beer and
    my stick.

v.

[You] are far down the road now
        other rocks in love with
        you

                      predictable.

SINCE 1783

Been conspiring to wash
the guts with knock-out
prices.

S'got a handsome hair-
cut, cool southern costumes
back at Prairie Land'll kill you,

deprive your worthless junk
the blood.

+

S'got a style says *come over! let's
fuck on pre-torn coupons yelling
"style for what!"*
Steals the aux cord bumping
millennial Jesus / Puts the bruises
in perspective.

PRAGMATISM

I know an Owl who knows
the rules / Finish your drink &

go before we end up raising
children.

I WILL WAKE UP TO A TEXT & HOOTS OF AN ALLEYWAY PIGEON

Early—   Sweaty duct &
Simple meaning ;;

                  a frozen plum \

neglected / or, possibly))

The exercise is patience and, by effect, a lot of patient
brewing. Tossing and soiling, entire
packs are smoked in single
thoughts of you.

What is this experiment? Why can I not
sleep without a program

                  what to hide from.

Why can I
not sleep?

JUST NOW

By the window, caring for a stupid bird
I lost it. Found myself a sprinter
in a fireplace all sealed up. Cutting boxes,
7Ws of natural light condensed to a single
picture frame. Ugly. Not defined enough to
comment. Not here just now but smoking
by the window

        not funny but I guess that's your opinion.

I never really cared but looked. Could never re-
define the need to stare at every feather
crooked. Didn't think enough about
the outcome.

Every single bird I know
is angry with me. Every single
window is a fucking prison.

LIKEWISE (FISH)

Anything they put in water

        terrified just sits
there flaccid, putty in a wet
slot. Epileptic / notes on learning

        how to fish with human
bone-parts. How to be another person

        altogether new.

The Fish don't think like that.
The Fish don't have to drink the city.

THE PARAMEDICS ACTED LIKE COPS
(to the old woman who fainted on Market Street)

Cold and unfriendly, with
terrible haircuts.

But I guess it's just
a stressful job.

CONSIDERING THE WINDOW

for Vera

I wear seven jackets inside and
Despise myself for blending patterns
Much more for watching porn without
Intention.

If there are metaphors in fruit-flies
I am a perverted piece of shit.

Nothing seems to die
the way it should.

PURSUANT TO THE CARD ISSUER AGREEMENT

for CA Conrad

Something I saw in a CEI video
her cello on a pile of letters
on her floor   the dynamism
of pussy

          strawberries
some Ammonal prepared by
gunslinger
                              goddesses of moss-
birds
and cigarettes tucked waistband
our golden children calling insanity the

Western standard.

ALBA

She mentioned to me morning weather
  clutching toward a whiskey stem.
I was offering to stay—to brush her hair
  after the orgasm.

An alba is supposed to be a song
of dawn,
  and unfaithful lovers
But when I try, I fail
to tap new rhythms on this
  sad and balding head.

WE PREFER A MORE ORIGINAL PEST

Than the damned fucking wind.
Than the blinds absorbing usual
Terrible habits.
Than an empty ice tray because I was tired
Of the outdoors.

Because I was sick of love and
Now find it only where it cannot
Will not last. When it strikes the skin
Of you running simple errands. When
You strike me and I fold because nothing
Helps at all, no matter. Because you are leaving
Anyway.

Like the wind. Who loves to watch
Me cursing nature. Who hates the peace and quiet
Sort of lovers. Who laughs as I walk backwards
Cursing everything. Who knows we sometimes want to die

and

Offers reasons. Who should not be allowed
To be invisible.

We want new low-grade suffering.
We want new seasons, altogether, entirely.

THE DANCER

Never leave aside
you angel-haired, you peach
this ramble

carried on in threes
and not the least bit, for the most part
ever happening

says *Go forward!* peach-hair'd
love and bring the dancer
back a wind chime / bring the dancer
back to claim her mail.

EXCEPTING THE PROCESS

She calls herself a water wheel then
folds into a vapor. Says she invented finger-paints
& Aristotle. "Warhol was a predator & a cunt."

I know the origins of Nothing so I
never need to beg some pressing Truth, or any
semblance of a better way to write things
down.   Listen like an old bat / I listen to a
                                        rolling bottle.

I'm still OK. I haven't learned a fucking thing
in years.

RESTRAINT

Take my love to your afterlife &
stop being so dramatic.

Take the book & press your lips
against it
                    filed in boxes.

Put it all down this time & finally
be patient with them / Never have a heart

       go writing poems.

SELF-HELP PORTRAIT

for Nicole

Picture a clown & picture a blue jay.
Picture being flopped around a single letter / addressed
to a vacant church pew on *A Patch of Woods*,
which is actually a name for something.

Picture the sign. Like a wooden cartoon or another
even less convincing instrument. A plastic harp or pale
horse tap-dancing on a toy piano. No real sounds just
perfect music. Several drunken minnows in a conga line.

This is how I see us: changing so abruptly as to
wake out of paralysis. Becoming this kaleidoscope of past
and now. Stripped and sober. Desperate just to infiltrate

               the stream :/ /

    I'm coming with you.
    I'm drilling us our cave into the mountain.

Picture all this happening. Picture the blue jay drinking
from an egg. Slurping up the neighborhood. Picture
our surprise as she protects them. Birds of prey, our love
is of this natural process. Innards by the talon of the mother hawk.

This is how I see us: feeding on an organ. Living as a
patch of rust and burning in the wood.

Picture a blue jay & picture a mime. Of course. What else but
always mirrors, fingerprints of a hit we never paid for &
in dreams. Of course. Picture a Self-Portrait:

    I am here and I am / *bloated*
    I am sorry and I am / *still so fucking hungry*

See the carpet now. Imagine you're a lonely
thread. Of course you're not. Don't listen to the poem.

Picture the blue jay.

Picture why you should be picturing the blue jay.

Because don't listen to the poem but not

        avoiding that you're in the thing / just
picturing the bird because you're sat down there just
drinking.

Because you're clicking keys and drinking from
the monkey cup. Because you're problematic otherwise

        no poem.

Nobody *needs* Authoritative Verse who doesn't
need it. You *need* to get fucked or you need a dollar ; you *need*
to call your mother on her birthday. Picture a clown.

Picture someone leaving and then
now you need it / Remember how we're still out

        in the *Patch of Woods*. The only name you've
ever heard make any sense at all.

Picture you accepting my apology for picturing
the blue jay.

Picture some more frightening dysmorphia. Your sunken
eyes two drum-points on a split branch. Tapping out these
church songs on the suffocating bodies of the fish. Those innards
now two yo-yos in a street performance. In *A Patch of Woods*.

You were *not* sorry.

You *are* not sorry.

But I feel sorry like a nail. I feel it like a
handle. I feel sorry like the water
in my piss. Like every calzone not to feel
dizzy / like masturbating.

I feel it like the warm of every swallow, like the
shatter of ceramics on the hardened dust. Like typical
imagery in poems, like perfect music.

I have put on boots too big for me and
thrown them on a coffee table, kicked back picturing
the picture on a screen and not picturing the
self-destruction melting in a mug / I have

        apologized.

I have written every single letter over

by itself / addressed to any faith or board
of critics worth addressing / I have

        realized my apologies all

blue and silver / red with little overthinking
blue jays in the wood.

I could go on.

I could apologize.

But picture all this happening.

DON'T EVER CRY

You told me don't ever cry, or else
your womb would fill with sand
and we'd be through.

You made me want to cry.

NO LONGER SHOULD THEY DIG THERE

Instead the letters pile up and
flower petals never move but sleep
as if reborn as open caskets.

Smaller people only visit, shorter
dreams more terrified than epics.

Their splayed out books remind them
not to dig there any longer. Their splayed out
bodies splinter'd by another letter.

Let the dead things rest
for once.

Let the things alone
to write.

RUSHING THE UN-LOVE

lady done inspired a
tail-spin.

        lady done
done   it—

        comes crawling back &
        fills an ice tray.

comes crawling
swims   & brand

new upholstery.

THE RUM DRAIN

Until the castles melt we
Exist here until the
Castles melt.

                    red barn washed
In white.

JERKING OFF ON THE WILDFIRE

We should've known / crying ghost &

shallow fire / metal hard & following instruction / yellow

girl who skips & hums /

                                             & swirling on the rink.

HOPE IT RAINS SO JELLY BIRD CAN SWIM

Hope it rains so Jelly Bird can swim.

Hope she bleeds in the next few days or

        canceling the great migration. Splashing

        in a constant circle.

Hope the rain is warmest like a bath.
Less ideal for breeding than for baptism.
Naked swimming legs that form an absence in
the spring and hold us there like sopping doves.

Hope it's silent.
Hope the blood comes rushing
like a scream

        warm and newborn / Paper wings alive

        and swimming.

Hope it's all a put-on. Hope it rains so Jelly Bird can
swim and no more tagging legs with plastic / arms against
her neck to trigger / a shaking of a wing

        hoping it rains so Jelly Bird is pleased
again. *Again , again , again* and
hope it's worth it. Hope Jelly Bird can smile and
count to thirty-one. Inspect the rain for catalysts of
birth defects

        newborn rain. Puddles for the shower now
and (*so on*). Losing out, becoming, or just prematurely
mourning the imaginary.

Hope Jelly Bird is pleased again. Folded
in a bed like some aesthetic / unnecessary

triangular pillow. Hope it's cozy there.

Hope the eyes develop first.
Hope they come to learn from
all the blood people.

Treading bubbles, scrub and
shine its open belly. Hoping she will call
and

                 disconfirm the temperature.

So Jelly Bird can swim.

So it won't be what the
poem's used to.

Solidifying the great migration,
and canceling the rain.

REVOLUTION ON VIBRATE

What we do to birds in poetry
They stage and mold for the social bell
And I do not fucking care anymore
How frustrated are the birds.

I am the worst poet
I have ever known.

I am the greatest poet
I have ever heard describe how much
You hate yourself.

NOTES ON AUTHORITATIVE VERSE

     Everything in its place. Nothing and everything with deliberation. The mints the spray. The prongs the magnet. The small green dots the bigger red one. Everything in its place with deliberation.

     Everything.
     Everything in its place.
     The books the basket. The glass the hat the water. Everything. The flowers the bone. The flesh the flowers the bone. Nothing and everything in its place.

                        The car the bag says *numbers*.
Nothing and everything))

     The car the bag. The card. Everything in its place. The window. The window with deliberation. The Jack the Blue Sky. The white the grey the mints. Nothing but the similar. And everything. And nothing with deliberation. The pants the slab the pyroclastic.

     But everything with deliberation.
     But everything and nothing with deliberation.

     But the beat, the slow the non-lethal. Nothing and everything with deliberation.

     The switch the magnet. The carpet feet.
     The jar the show the wood-
pecker. Nothing.

     Everything in its place with deliberation. The shares. The flesh the flowers. The magnet with deliberation. The Blue the black. The skates the nose. Nothing but the bone. And everything. Similar. And nothing.

     The walk the check.
     The wall the handle. The
     wood the brick and everything with deliberation. The print the sale. The stress the bone the pyroclastic. The bank the plant. The center with deliberation. The bright the new. The state the care and nothing with deliberation. Everything in its place.

     The bull the stare.
     The pill the magnet.
     The pink the Blue. The sad
     the new and everything with deliberation.

     The girl they call the elbows.

The stone the lift. The small blue dots the bigger
red one with deliberation.

Everything. The knob the candle. The large green bone.
Everything and nothing with deliberation.

The bone the magnet. The state the plant. The spoon the show
the syntax with deliberation. The bug the feather. The wind the ash the
bone the magnet. The flowers. Nothing and everything with
deliberation. The phone the shoe the girl they call the elbows.
Everything.

        Take (this: say "silent") momentum
        and place it

        there.

Everything in its place. Everything and nothing with
deliberation. The cup the laugh the mints. The card the pen and
everything with deliberation. The moment lost the card the dime. The
check the list the strike the (d)one. Nothing. Nothing and everything
with deliberation. The hands the maps the letter. The letter. The letter
with deliberation. Everything in its place. The brick the stripe.

    The stripe the bone.
    The table with deliberation.
    The wet the cold the stone the
    bark and nothing.

        (this) the reverse)

    The skyline with deliberation.
    The shape the new the
    elbow. The shapes the news
    the wet-cold with deliberation.

Everything in its place.
Everything in its place and everything with deliberation. And
nothing. (The J the N the C. The deconstructed.) The horse the yellow.
The Blue the post the symptoms with deliberation. The coarse the
never-ending. The use the shell the void if nothing. The knot if nothing
and everything with deliberation. The prongs the magnet. The bone the
blood.

    The exhaustive. The
    shell the pipe the
    bone. Everything in its
                    place))

The score. The flesh the flower/s magnet.

                       the hook the hat the shore: Everything :: Nothing and Everything)))

         Everything with deliberation. Everything in its place. The snow the filter. The bone the flower/s magnet. The coarse the never-ending.

         Everything. The stop the pull the gas. The harsh the man-made. The blood the bone the tiger with deliberation. The fish the floor the mud. (And nothing.) The mat the heat the bone again. The coarse the shell the magnet with deliberation. The false the score. The skyline. The news the nothing. The place the pipe and everything. Everything in its place. (The T the S.) The switch the card the mattress with deliberation. The mattress. The dime the coast the elbow. Nothing. The speed the club the speed the club. Everything.

         The speed the club.
         The bone the magnet. The
         score the pump the
         hand the table. Everything in its
         place. The hat the rib the
         bone. The face the blood the cup
         the table. The wrap the switch the
         plug the bone. The magnet. Everything
         in its place. The sport the yellow. The
         Blue the news the pyroclastic. The
         plug the small green dots the bigger
         red one. The rap the seen the scene the
         elbow. Everything. Everything and nothing
         in its place. The mood. The mood the snow the
         plug the bone. Nothing and everything in its place.

         The farm the
         front the
                 skyline :: pyro-
                 clastic)) place this

                                       there.

         (Everything) in its place. Nothing and everything with deliberation. The heart the strong the syntax. The similar. The similar and nothing with deliberation. And everything.

         And everything.
         And everything.
         And everything and nothing with deliberation.
         And everything with deliberation.

And everything.
And everything in its place / /

www.ingramcontent.com/pod-product-compliance
Lightning Source LLC
Chambersburg PA
CBHW060507080526
44584CB00015B/1586